THE OFFICIAL
Arsenal
ANNUAL 2013

Written by Chas Newkey-Burden
(with additional research by Daniel Paull)

Designed by Brian Thomson

A Grange Publication

ISBN 978-1-908925-00-8

£7.99

CONTENTS

MANAGER'S MESSAGE

Welcome to the Official Arsenal Annual 2013. There is so much to enjoy in this year's edition, including all the essential facts, stats and photographs of the 2011/12 season. There are also puzzles, posters and much more to keep every Gunners fan entertained.

What an eventful campaign 2011/12 was: we lost four of the first seven Premier League fixtures and yet we kept our composure, worked hard together and finished in third place. The squad grew in strength, belief and experience as the season progressed and created an optimism amongst the fans again.

Some of our performances in the Champions League, particularly the victories against Udinese and Borussia Dortmund, were very satisfying. So was the second-leg against AC Milan in the same competition, when we showed our strength, energy and determination to respond magnificently to a heavy deficit only to fall agonisingly short.

Domestically, our thrilling victories over Chelsea, Tottenham Hotspur and Blackburn Rovers will be remembered for some time.

With a young, talented squad being joined by some significant new signings, we believe that we are now in a good position to challenge strongly for honours in the near future.

On behalf of everyone at the Club I would like to thank you for your continued support, which inspires us all during and between games.

Enjoy the Official Arsenal Annual 2013!

Arsène Wenger

PREMIER LEAGUE REVIEW

A season that started with a string of disappointing results ended with The Gunners in third place – a position many would have thought impossible during the opening two months of the campaign. There were a number of fine performances and memorable victories during the Premier League season. Here follows the story of 2011/12 in the League...

August

The opening month of the Premier League campaign was tough for all concerned with Arsenal. In the course of August's three league ties, the Gunners amassed just one point, scored three goals and conceded 10. In truth, the fixture list had dealt the Club a tricky trio of matches to open the campaign with, and it showed.

The first of the trio came in the form of a trip to the north-east to face Newcastle United. The Gunners dominated the first 75 minutes of the match and seemed a fair bet to convert their supremacy into three points. Walcott and Van Persie had already come very close to scoring. However, when Gervinho was sent off, it robbed the match of a grandstand finish.

Seven days later, Wenger's side hosted Liverpool. Again, a Gunner was to see red during the match but this time the team finished as the losing side. The score-line does scant justice to the run of play in a tie that Arsenal performed brilliantly in. It was only after Emmanuel Frimpong's dismissal that Liverpool nicked two goals.

The Gunners arrived at Old Trafford hit by injuries and suspensions. They left humbled, having been defeated 8-2 by a rampant United side. Goals from Walcott and Van Persie scarcely lightened the mood, yet the faithful singing and chanting of the visiting fans showed true class.

13	Newcastle United 0-0 Arsenal	
20	Arsenal 0-2 Liverpool	
28	Manchester United 8-2 Arsenal	
	(Walcott, Van Persie)	

September

The Gunners recorded their first League win of the season against Swansea City. The decisive strike came five minutes before the half-time break from Andrey Arshavin. The Russian received the ball from a misjudged Swansea throw-in and stabbed it home from a narrow angle. This proved the highlight of the match but the precious three points were confirmed by the final whistle.

As the teams broke for half-time at Ewood Park a week later, Arsenal were 2-1 ahead thanks to goals from Gervinho and Arteta. However, an own goal from Song after the break turned the match on its head. By the time Chamakh made it three for Arsenal, Blackburn had already netted four times and sewn up the win.

Back at Emirates Stadium, Arsenal beat Bolton Wanderers 3-0. The pick of the action came in the shape of Van Persie's 100th goal for the Club. The Dutchman scored two on the day and was joined on the score-sheet by Song, who curled home a beauty in the 89th minute. A clean sheet, three points and a century of goals for Van Persie – it was a happy afternoon for Gunners fans.

10 **Arsenal 1-0 Swansea** *(Arshavin)*

17 **Blackburn Rovers 4-3 Arsenal**
   (Gervinho, Arteta, Chamakh)

24 **Arsenal 3-0 Bolton Wanderers**
   (Van Persie 2, Song)

October

Sandwiched between two dramatic London derbies came a pair of home wins for the Gunners in a month in which the results were the very definition of 'mixed fortunes'. A contentious goal from Rafael van der Vaart at White Hart Lane was equalised by Aaron Ramsey's close range strike. However, Arsenal's local rivals went on to win a frenetic derby.

The next two matches were both at home and the Gunners won them both. A pair of Van Persie goals – the first coming in the opening minute – gave Arsenal a welcome victory against Sunderland. His late winner was raucously greeted. The Dutchman again struck twice, with Gervinho also on the score-sheet, at home to Stoke City a week later.

A third successive victory was achieved at the end of an eventful, eight-goal tie at Stamford Bridge. Although Chelsea led 2-1 at the break, by full-time a hat-trick from the rampant Van Persie, together with Santos and Walcott goals, gave the Gunners a 5-3 victory. The disappointments of August and September were replaced by excitement and joy.

02 **Tottenham Hotspur 2-1 Arsenal** (Ramsey)

16 **Arsenal 2-1 Sunderland** (Van Persie 2)

23 **Arsenal 3-1 Stoke City** (Gervinho, Van Persie 2)

29 **Chelsea 3-5 Arsenal**
(Van Persie 3, Santos, Walcott)

November

After three wins on the trot in October, the Gunners needed to keep their fine form flowing. They did just that during an unbeaten November. At Emirates Stadium, Wenger's team comfortably beat West Bromwich Albion, with Arteta and Vermaelen among the goal-scorers. The carefully kept clean sheet was also welcome.

Van Persie, who had scored one and set-up two against West Brom, netted twice at Carrow Road as the team came back from 1-0 down to beat Norwich City 2-1. The victory was richly deserved, with Arsenal in fluent and imperious form. There were smiles all round in the visitors' stand.

Thomas Vermaelen scored twice against Fulham back at Emirates Stadium – once for each team. The Belgian defender had given the visitors a surprise lead with his 65th-minute own goal. He atoned heroically with a headed equaliser in the 85th minute.

December

A comprehensive victory on the road is always a joy. Wenger's heroes grabbed one of them with a 4-0 win at Wigan in the first match of December. Arteta and Vermaelen opened the scoring in the first half. By the time Gervinho and Van Persie collectively doubled the lead in the second half, the match was Arsenal's.

Another three points were claimed at home to Everton a week later. With 20 minutes left, Van Persie clipped home a fine shot from 20 yards. It was a strike more than worthy of putting the Gunners into the top four for the first time in the campaign. Then came Arsenal's first defeat since the start of October, in the shape of a 1-0 loss at Manchester City.

The final three Premier League ties of 2011 sent seven points the Gunners' way. Yossi Benayoun scored a late winner at Villa Park. Gervinho scored Arsenal's goal in a 1-1 draw at home to Wolves, and the striker of 2011, Van Persie, netted the winner against QPR in the Club's final match of the calendar year.

03 **Wigan Athletic 0-4 Arsenal**
(Arteta, Vermaelen, Gervinho, Van Persie)

10 **Arsenal 1-0 Everton** (Van Persie)

18 **Manchester City 1-0 Arsenal**

21 **Aston Villa 1-2 Arsenal**
(Van Persie, Benayoun)

27 **Arsenal 1-1 Wolverhampton Wanderers**
(Gervinho)

31 **Arsenal 1-0 Queens Park Rangers**
(Van Persie)

January

The results for January make for depressing reading for any Gunner: played three, lost three. At Craven Cottage Bobby Zamora gave Fulham a late win in an eventful tie. Koscielny had scored the opener before a denied penalty, a red card, and a goal from former Gunner Sidwell, changed the complexion of the game.

Although both Van Persie and Walcott were on target at Swansea, the Gunners lost again – their seventh defeat of the season to date. The prospects for the Club's first match in the city for 20 years had seemed so promising when the Dutchman had given them a fifth-minute lead.

Victory against Manchester United would have been just the tonic for Arsenal at this point – and they so nearly achieved it. After the visitors took the lead on half-time, the Gunners mounted a second-half revival that peaked with Van Persie's 71st-minute goal. However, Danny Welbeck broke Gunners' hearts with his late winner.

02 Fulham 2-1 Arsenal *(Koscielny)*

15 Swansea 3-2 Arsenal *(Van Persie, Walcott)*

22 Arsenal 1-2 Manchester United *(Van Persie)*

February

After a goalless draw in the first match of February, the red-hot Gunners scored 14 goals in three matches. Although Van Persie hit the woodwork twice at Bolton, neither side were able to find the back of the net.

How different it was against Blackburn at Emirates Stadium just three days later. A Van Persie hat-trick formed the heart of a 7-1 win that also saw Oxlade-Chamberlain net twice. An own goal from Scott Dann and an Arteta strike completed the walloping win.

A comparatively goal-shy 2-1 win over Sunderland a week later was secured with a last-gasp winner from the returned hero, Thierry Henry. He sent home Andrey Arshavin's wonderful cross in the dying seconds. Then, the Gunners beat Tottenham 5-2. The victory was all the sweeter for the fact that Spurs had gone 2-0 up, before a sensational comeback – spearheaded by a brace from Walcott – made the day Arsenal's.

01 **Bolton Wanders 0-0 Arsenal**

04 **Arsenal 7-1 Blackburn Rovers**
(Van Persie 3, Oxlade-Chamberlain 2, Arteta, Dan [og])

11 **Sunderland 1-2 Arsenal** *(Ramsey, Henry)*

26 **Arsenal 5-2 Tottenham Hotspur**
(Sagna, Van Persie, Rosicky, Walcott 2)

March

Fans of comebacks were enjoying themselves as the Gunners pulled off another at Anfield. Having gone 1-0 down through a Koscielny own goal, Arsenal beat Liverpool with two Van Persie strikes. The crucial goal was the Dutchman's 25th of the campaign.

His 26th game against Newcastle United and – together with Vermaelen's – earned the red-and-white heroes another win. Vermaelen was on target again at Goodison Park. His early header took Arsenal into third place.

They tightened their grip on that position with a three-goal win over Aston Villa. Kieran Gibbs was among the goals in their seventh victory in a row – the Club's best run since October 2007. That run came to an end with defeat at Queens Park Rangers. Theo Walcott's goal – fired in from the rebound – was sandwiched between two from the home side.

03 **Liverpool 1-2 Arsenal** *(Van Persie 2)*

12 **Arsenal 2-1 Newcastle United**
   (Van Persie, Vermaelen)

21 **Everton 0-1 Arsenal** *(Vermaelen)*

24 **Arsenal 3-0 Aston Villa**
   (Gibbs, Walcott, Arteta)

31 **Queens Park Rangers 2-1 Arsenal** *(Walcott)*

April

With just three minutes left at home to Manchester City, Mikel Arteta struck home from 25 yards out. It was a worthy and deserved winner, as the Gunners had dominated the match. Robin Van Persie and Theo Walcott had both hit the woodwork during an impressive afternoon.

By the 12th minute of the match at Wolves, the visitors were already in charge of the tie. A sixth-minute penalty from Van Persie was followed by a strong goal from the edge of the area by Walcott. Benayoun added a third in the second-half. This win took Arsenal five points clear of fourth-placed Tottenham.

By the time Vermaelen headed home in the 21st minute against Wigan, the opponents had already netted twice. As it turned out, the Belgian's goal was to be a mere consolation in the Club's third home defeat of the Premier League season. Chelsea were the next visitors to Emirates Stadium. This time, in contrast to the eight-goal thriller at Stamford Bridge, the match finished goalless.

The final match of the month was against Stoke and ended in a 1-1 draw, with Van Persie scoring his 28th league goal of the campaign. With just two matches left, the Gunners were determined to secure qualification to the Champions League.

08 **Arsenal 1-0 Manchester City** *(Arteta)*

11 **Wolverhampton Wanderers 0-3 Arsenal**
(Van Persie, Benayoun, Walcott)

16 **Arsenal 1-2 Wigan Athletic** *(Vermaelen)*

21 **Arsenal 0-0 Chelsea**

28 **Stoke City 1-1 Arsenal** *(Van Persie)*

May

With just 10 minutes left on the clock at Emirates Stadium, the Gunners were leading Norwich City 3-2. They were worth their lead, which had been first achieved just 65 seconds into the match via Benayoun. However, in the 85th minute Norwich equalised. This meant the Gunners would have to wait until the final weekend to know if they would qualify for the Champions League.

At West Brom, Arsenal did indeed secure that qualification – but not without a bit of drama. Benayoun opened the scoring early, but after 16 minutes the team trailed 2-1. Santos and Koscielny scored a goal each to grab a final three points from

During the testing opening months of the campaign, a third-placed finish would have seemed unlikely for Arsenal. However, the squad stuck together and worked hard. Their quality and dedication increasingly shone through. Here's to the future.

05 **Arsenal 3-3 Norwich City**
   (Benayoun, Van Persie 2)

13 **West Bromwich Albion 2-3 Arsenal**
   (Benayoun, Santos, Koscielny)

PLAYER PROFILES

WOJCIECH SZCZESNY

Born: April 18, 1990
Warsaw, Poland
Squad number: 13
Position: Goalkeeper
Joined Gunners: August 01, 2007

a n ever-present during the Premier League campaign of 2011/12, Szczesny has more than fulfilled Arsène Wenger's longstanding faith in him. The prescient Manager predicted in 2010: *"I believe one day he will be the No 1 at Arsenal, certainly."*

After joining the Club from Legia Warsaw, the Pole was given a loan spell at Brentford. He made his Gunners league debut at Old Trafford in 2010. He immediately displayed his characteristically assured, composed style of play.

An injury to his fellow countryman Lukasz Fabianski then gave him a longer run in the side, which he seized as expertly as he seizes the ball when he is between the sticks.

A commanding and reassuring figure on the pitch, he has become one of Europe's most respected custodians. One Gunners fan even described him as 'the goalie version of Lionel Messi'. Praise indeed.

WOJCIECH SAYS: *"It's always satisfying to hear people praising you, but I'm at the beginning of my career with a long way to go. I'm looking forward to playing for this Club for a long, long time. I'm just trying to do my best for the Club."*

ARSÈNE WENGER SAYS:

He has improved in his focus, the consistency of it. The talent was always there but he is maturing quickly. I like that he is a good communicator. You have to adjust, it's important to find a balance. The mental part of a keeper is vital.

THOMAS VERMAELEN

Born: November 14, 1985
Kapellen, Belgium

Squad number: 5

Position: Defender

Joined Gunners: June 19, 2009

f ew in England had heard of Thomas when he arrived from Ajax in the summer of 2009 – but once he pulled on an Arsenal shirt everyone sat up and took notice of this commanding defender. He quickly made a name for himself thanks to his fine tackling and decisive style of play.

He is also a threat in attack, scoring eight goals in his first season in England, including long-range shots against Blackburn Rovers and Wigan Athletic that were worthy of a striker. He was named vice captain in 2011, recognition of his masterful presence in the team: if you were in a war you would want the Belgian international on your side.

He has made clear that his priority remains his defensive duties, rather than his contributions in attack. Expect this phenomenal and formidable footballer – who has been described as *"an absolute soldier"* by Theo Walcott – to become an ever more influential player for the Gunners.

THOMAS SAYS: *"When the boss made me vice-captain it made me proud. I am really happy to be vice-captain of such a big club like Arsenal. I feel the responsibility to help the captain in his role as well, and of course that means the Club and the boss give you a lot of confidence."*

ARSÈNE WENGER SAYS:

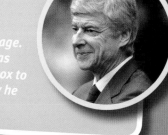

66 *Thomas and Arsenal have a happy marriage. He has been absolutely vital for us. As well as being a fine defender, he has a nose in the box to find a goal where it is needed and I must say he is a good finisher.* 99

CHAMPIONS LEAGUE

Arsenal v Udinese

The Gunners started the campaign with an impressive 1-0 in the first-leg of the Champions League play-off against Udinese. Theo Walcott scored the winner in the fourth minute of the tie, sending home an Aaron Ramsey pass at the near post. He celebrated in style with a golf swing movement. Both sides had further chances but were unable to convert them.

EURO FACT: *This was the Club's second successive clean sheet.*

Udinese v Arsenal

Walcott was on target again in the second-leg in northern Italy. So was Van Persie, whose 55th minute strike equalised Udinese's first-half opener. The Dutchman's strike completed fine build-up work from Gervinho, whereas Walcott's strike came as part of a breakaway. This confirmed a 3-1 aggregate win for the Gunners.

EURO FACT: *This was the 14th successive season in which Arsenal reached the group stages of the Champions League.*

Borussia Dortmund v Arsenal

Wenger's team came so agonisingly close to winning in Germany. Three minutes before the half-time break, Van Persie lashed the ball home to give the Gunners a deserved lead. The team then defended resolutely to protect their lead, which lasted until the 88th minute. Ivan Perisic struck the equaliser to break Arsenal hearts.

EURO FACT: *Israeli international Yossi Benayoun made his Arsenal debut in this match.*

Arsenal v Olympiacos

The Greek champions were in fine fettle in north London, yet Arsenal finished the match on top. Oxlade-Chamberlain and Santos both pounced in the first half, before a header from David Fuster handed the visitors a lifeline. Despite concerted energy and pressure from Olympiacos – including a curler from Vassilis Torossidis that hit the bar – Arsenal held onto their lead.

EURO FACT: *Alex Oxlade-Chamberlain's goal made him the Club's youngest ever scorer in the competition.*

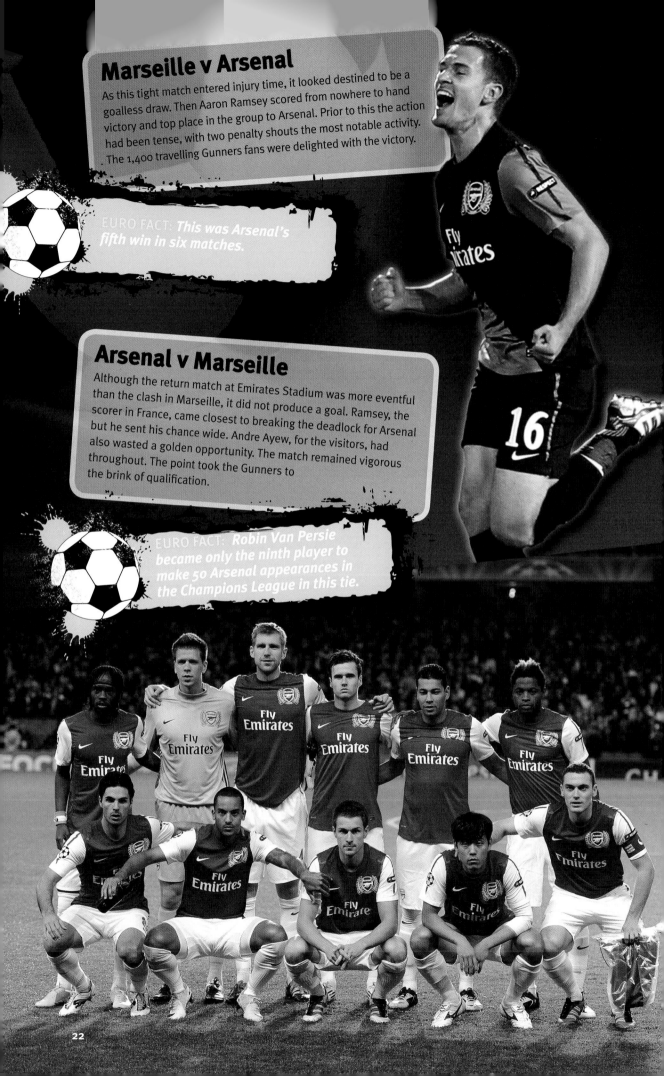

Marseille v Arsenal

As this tight match entered injury time, it looked destined to be a goalless draw. Then Aaron Ramsey scored from nowhere to hand victory and top place in the group to Arsenal. Prior to this the action had been tense, with two penalty shouts the most notable activity. The 1,400 travelling Gunners fans were delighted with the victory.

EURO FACT: **This was Arsenal's fifth win in six matches.**

Arsenal v Marseille

Although the return match at Emirates Stadium was more eventful than the clash in Marseille, it did not produce a goal. Ramsey, the scorer in France, came closest to breaking the deadlock for Arsenal but he sent his chance wide. Andre Ayew, for the visitors, had also wasted a golden opportunity. The match remained vigorous throughout. The point took the Gunners to the brink of qualification.

EURO FACT: *Robin Van Persie became only the ninth player to make 50 Arsenal appearances in the Champions League in this tie.*

Arsenal v Borussia Dortmund

Two goals from captain Van Persie fired Arsenal into the next round of the Champions League. The pick of the pair was his opener, in which he converted a fine assist from Alex Song. Although Shinji Kagawa struck a consolation with the last kick of the game, the home side took the points and the glory. Arsenal were in fine form in Europe again.

EURO FACT: *This was the 12th successive campaign in which the Gunners have reached the knock-out stages of the Champions League.*

Olympiacos v Arsenal

With qualification secured, Wenger shuffled the pack for the final group game. A youthful Gunners side gained useful experience of European competition, despite the defeat. Yossi Benayoun scored the visitors' only goal – a superb volley on the hour. The Greeks, still chasing qualification, were in testing form. They failed to achieve that, due to results elsewhere, but the Gunners marched on.

EURO FACT: *This was Arsène Wenger's 200th game in European competition.*

23

AC Milan v Arsenal

Although Robin Van Persie forced Milan goalkeeper Christian Abbiati into two fine saves, the home side fully deserved to win this tie. Perhaps the 4-0 score-line flattered Milan slightly, but the Gunners simply did not do enough to challenge in this match. By the time Zlatan Ibrahimovic made it four for Milan eleven minutes from time, few would have given Arsenal a chance of giving Milan a fright in the second-leg in north London.

EURO FACT: This was the final match of Thierry Henry's second spell at the Club.

Arsenal v AC Milan

Laurent Koscielny's seventh-minute header served notice early on that the Gunners fully intended to fight all the way for their European lives. Twenty minutes later Rosicky doubled the lead. Suddenly, everyone began to believe that the Gunners had a whiff of a chance of reversing the four-goal deficit. By half-time, Van Persie had made it three from the penalty spot. That, though, turned out to be the final goal of the tie and of Arsenal's European campaign.

EURO FACT: A comeback from a four-goal deficit had only been achieved three times in the history of the competition.

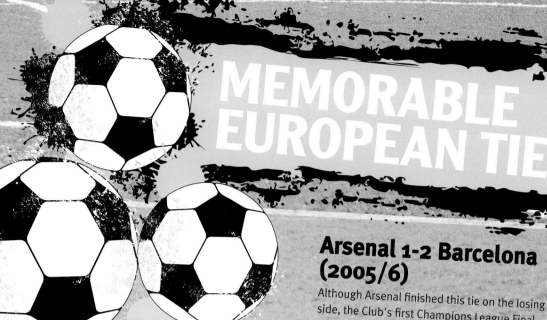

MEMORABLE EUROPEAN TIES

Arsenal 1-2 Barcelona (2005/6)

Although Arsenal finished this tie on the losing side, the Club's first Champions League Final remains a key moment in the Gunners history books. Sol Campbell scored for Wenger's side.

Inter Milan 1-5 Arsenal (2003/4)

The score-line almost says it all. The pick of Arsenal's fantastic five goals came from Thierry Henry, who capped a fine move by crashing the ball home in off the post.

Real Madrid 0-1 Arsenal (2005/6)

Two minutes into the second-half, Fabregas found Henry in the centre circle. The Frenchman then won the tie with a superb solo goal. Arsenal became the first English team to beat Real Madrid on their own patch.

Arsenal 2-0 Juventus (2005/6)

The Gunners beat the Italian giants at Highbury, with Cesc Fabregas setting-up one goal and scoring another, to eclipse the returning former Gunner Patrick Vieira.

AC Milan 0-2 Arsenal (2007/8)

Fabregas broke the deadlock with just six minutes left with a fine 20-yard strike. Emmanuel Adebayor added a second in the final minute to send the Gunners to the quarter final.

16 August 2011
Arsenal 1-0 Udinese (Walcott)

24 August 2011
Udinese 1-2 Arsenal (Van Persie, Walcott)

13 September 2011
Borussia Dortmund 1-1 Arsenal (Van Persie)

28 September 2011
Arsenal 2-1 Olympiacos
(Oxlade-Chamberlain, Santos)

19 October 2011
Arsenal 1-0 Marseille (Ramsey)

1 November 2011
Marseille 0-0 Arsenal

23 November 2011
Arsenal 2-1 Borussia Dortmund (Van Persie 2)

6 December 2011
Olympiacos 3-1 Arsenal (Benayoun)

15 February 2012
AC Milan 4-0 Arsenal

6 March 2012
Arsenal 3-0 AC Milan
(Koscielny, Rosicky, Van Persie)

TOP 10 GOALS OF THE SEASON

In a season packed with sensational strikes, here are 10 of the best. From late winners to long-range beauties via miraculous volleys, this is a truly wondrous collection of Gunners goals.

Thierry Henry
v Sunderland, February 11

In the final Premier League match of his second Arsenal career, the Frenchman secured a last-gasp win. In the dying minutes of the match, Andrey Arshavin sent in two fine crosses. The first was headed straight at the goalkeeper by Van Persie. The second was stabbed home by Henry.

Robin Van Persie
v Tottenham Hotspur, February 26

The jewel in the crown of arguably the greatest comeback in Arsenal history was Van Persie's goal in the 43rd minute. Standing just outside the area he struck the ball with his left foot. His shot curled into the top corner and levelled the score-line.

Tomas Rosicky
v Tottenham Hotspur, February 26

This strike sent Arsenal ahead in the north London derby. Rosicky, who had worked tirelessly throughout the match, was on hand to magnificently send home a cross from the overlapping Sagna. It was the Czech's first league goal of the season and the fans greeted it with an almost deafening roar.

Robin Van Persie
v Liverpool, March 3

In the wake of this match, Theo Walcott said it was "a dream" to play with Robin Van Persie. For the fans, it was a dream to watch the Dutchman. In the last minute of this match, with the score level at 1-1, Van Persie converted an exquisite pass from Song into a side-foot shot that whizzed past Reina at his near post. Thanks to this sublime strike, Arsenal became the first team to win at Anfield in the season to date.

Theo Walcott
v Chelsea, October 29

The Englishman's 55th-minute goal crystallised Arsenal's comeback in this pulsating derby. Collecting the ball on the right-hand side, he soared infield. As he neared the penalty box he stumbled over, leading the Chelsea defence to wonder if the danger was over. Walcott returned quickly to his feet, weaved past a few opponents and lashed the ball home.

Mikel Arteta
v Manchester City, April 8

As the match seemed destined to finish goalless, the Spaniard decided otherwise. In the 87th minute he pinched possession from David Pizarro, powered forward and then unleashed a 25-yard shot that left Joe Hart powerless. This was the second successive home match that had been graced by a long-range goal from Arteta.

Robin Van Persie
v Everton, December 10

This was a goal that won the match and sent the Gunners into the top four for the first time in the campaign. Its significance was matched by its beauty. With 20 minutes left, Van Persie connected with a clipped cross-field pass from Song. He sent it volleying into the back of the net.

Mikael Arteta
v West Brom

Here, Robin Van Persie showed once again that as well as scoring goals he can also set them up. Having opened the scoring in the first half, in the 74th minute the Dutchman delicately passed the ball back to Arteta who majestically swept it into the opposition net from the edge of the penalty area. It was his first goal at Emirates Stadium.

Alex Oxlade-Chamberlain
v Shrewsbury, September 20

Arsenal players always remember their first goal for the Club. When those goals are as breathtaking as Oxlade-Chamberlain's debut strike was, the fans remember them too. Just before the hour, the 18-year-old received the ball and thumped it home from fully 25 yards out. It was such a powerful shot that Ben Smith could only watch as it bounced off him and into the net.

Yossi Benayoun
v Olympiacos, December 6

A youthful Gunners side lost this tie in Greece 3-1. The disappointment of the result was eased by the brilliance of Benayoun's consolation strike. Miquel's cross was eased on by Chamakh, and Benayoun struck an effort that went across the goalkeeper and into the far corner of the net.

A HISTORY OF THE SILVERWARE

What better way to tell the proud history of Arsenal Football Club than via the many trophies the Club has won? This glittering story of delicious doubles, fine FA Cup finals, and terrific titles, is enough to thrill any Gunners fan.

1930

1930:
Arsenal win the FA Cup, beating Huddersfield Town 2-0 at Wembley Stadium. Alex James and Jack Lambert were the scorers. The match was notable for the fact that Gunners Manager Herbert Chapman had previously managed Huddersfield Town, and for the appearance of the Graf Zeppelin German airship over the stadium during the match.

In the same year, the Gunners land their first Charity Shield, beating Sheffield Wednesday 2-1.

1931:
Arsenal crowned League Champions, collecting a record 66 points. They were the first Southern club to win the trophy.

1933:
Arsenal crowned Champions again.

1934:
A second successive Championship for the Gunners, their third overall.

1935:
George Allison at the helm as Arsenal win a third successive title.

1935

1936

1936:
A goal from Ted Drake wins the Gunners their second FA Cup, against Sheffield United.

1938:
Arsenal win their seventh major honour of the decade, beating Wolves and Brentford to the Championship.

1948:
Tom Whittaker guides Arsenal to the Championship in his first season in charge.

1948

1950:
Wearing unfamiliar gold jerseys does not prevent Arsenal from beating Liverpool in the FA Cup Final. Reg Lewis scored both Gunners goals.

1953:
Arsenal win another League Championship, pipping Preston to the title thanks to goal average.

1950

1970:
Seventeen years without trophies comes to an end when Arsenal beat Anderlecht in the European Fairs Cup Final.

1971:
Bertie Mee's Gunners win the League and FA Cup double – only the second Club to do so in the 20th century. Charlie George's extra-time winner at Wembley against Liverpool caps one of the Club's finest ever seasons.

1979:
An epic FA Cup Final ends with the Gunners beating Manchester United 3-2, thanks to a late winner from Alan Sunderland.

1987:
The Gunners beat Liverpool 2-1 in the League Cup Final - the first trophy of the George Graham era.

1989:
In arguably the greatest climax to a League campaign, Arsenal travelled to Anfield, needing to win the game by two goals win the title. After Alan Smith opened the scoring in the second-half, a last-minute Mickey Thomas strike lands the Club its first League Championship for 18 years.

1991:
The Gunners lose just one match as they win their second League title under George Graham. The wonderfully miserly defence concedes a mere 18 goals.

1970

1970

1987

1989

1993:
Arsenal becomes the first Club to win both domestic cups after beating Sheffield Wednesday in the finals of the FA and League cups.

1994:
The trophies keep coming under Graham's reign: this time the Gunners win the European Cup Winners' Cup, beating Italian giants Parma 1-0.

1998:
In new Manager Arsene Wenger's first full season at the helm, the Club wins the League and Cup double. Goals from Nicolas Anelka and Marc Overmars overcome Newcastle United in the FA Cup Final at Wembley.

2002:
Arsenal win the second double of Wenger's reign. The Premier League is secured at Old Trafford and the FA Cup Final sees Ray Parlour and Freddie Ljungberg net against Chelsea.

2004:
Setting a new Club record with 90 points, The Gunners win the Premier League after going through an entire League season without defeat. The squad is acclaimed as 'The Invincibles'.

2005:
The Gunners win the FA Cup again after beating Manchester United 5-4 on penalties after a 0-0 draw.

To be continued...

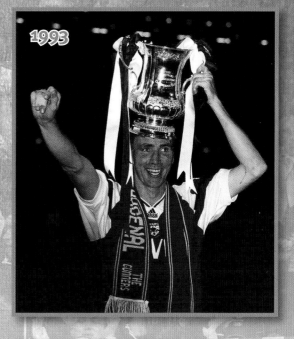

1993

1998

2005

FA CUP REVIEW

5th Round

Arsenal v Sunderland

Arsenal went into this tie off the back of a 4-0 defeat at AC Milan. The legacy of that disappointment was seen in at the Stadium of Light. Although both Sunderland goals were lucky, the home side did deserve their victory at the end of a wholehearted cup tie. The visiting fans, who were ushered to the north-east in £5 coaches Arsenal had laid on, saw Mikel Arteta, Gervinho and Robin Van Persie come close to scoring. However, it was Sunderland who found the net: first, through a Kieran Richardson deflection and then with an own goal by Alex Oxlade-Chamberlain.

Match fact: Francis Coquelin became the third Arsenal defender in three matches to leave the pitch through injury.

FA Cup Winners (10)

2005 Beat Man Utd 5-4 pens
       (after 0-0 draw, aet)

2003 Beat Southampton 1-0

2002 Beat Chelsea 2-0

1998 Beat Newcastle United 2-0

1993 Beat Sheff Weds 2-1
       (aet, replay after 1-1 draw)

1979 Beat Manchester United 3-2

1971 Beat Liverpool 2-1 (aet)

1950 Beat Liverpool 2-0

1936 Beat Sheffield United 1-0

1930 Beat Huddersfield Town 2-0

3rd Round
Arsenal v Leeds United

Match fact: This was the second successive year that the Gunners had faced Leeds United in the Third Round.

This tie will forever be remembered as Thierry Henry's night. The returning Frenchman entered the fray in the 68th minute when he replaced Marouane Chamakh. The cheers that greeted Henry's arrival on the pitch were of the volume usually received for a winning goal, rather than a substitution. Just 10 minutes later Henry provided the winner when he pulled away from his marker, commanded Alex Song's penetrating pass and slid the ball into the far corner. It was an intelligent move of the kind he had graced games with throughout his main Arsenal career.

4th Round
Arsenal v Aston Villa

If you go into the half-time break two goals down in the FA Cup, there is no better response in the second-half than scoring three goals in seven minutes. Robin Van Persie netted two of those goals from the penalty spot, with a goal from Theo Walcott sandwiched in between. The fans erupted as the Dutchman celebrated the winner. It had been a courageous and determined comeback from the Gunners, who trailed the visitors at half-time due to goals from Richard Dunne and Darren Bent. Having surrendered their lead, Aston Villa were not allowed back into the game by a resurgent Arsenal, who could have added more goals in the closing minutes.

Match fact: Villa had lost just twice on the road in the Premier League prior to this tie.

NEW SIGNINGS

Olivier Giroud

Born: *September 30, 1986, Chambery, France*

Position: *Striker*

Squad Number: *12*

Previous Clubs: *Montpellier, Tours, Istres, Montpellier*

Joined Arsenal: *July 01, 2012*

A lofty presence in the Gunners attack, 6ft 3in Olivier is a fine addition to the squad. He joined the Club on the back of a superb season at Montpellier, in which he had scored 25 goals in just 43 matches. He then went on to appear for France at the Euro 2012 tournament.

Beginning his career at Grenoble, he has also played for Istres and Tours, where he played alongside future Gunner Laurent Koscielny, before moving to Montpellier. He is a bright, fast and deadly striker, who is also fervent in the central pastures, where he contributes well to build-up play.

Santi Cazorla

Born: *December 13, 1984, Llanera, Spain*

Position: *Midfielder*

Squad Number: *19*

Previous Clubs: *Malaga, Villarreal, Recreativo, Villarreal, Oviedo*

Joined Arsenal: *August 07, 2012*

Spanish international Santi has shown himself to be an artistic and powerful presence in the midfield of many a football match. Agile, clever and creatively gifted, he can play in a number of positions in the midfield. He is lethal from set-pieces, and can score as well as create, goals.

A member of Spain's victorious squads at the 2008 and 2012 European Championships, his experience at club and country level will be a fine addition to the Gunners squad. Santi, who was voted Spanish Player of the Year in 2007, is a player to watch.

Lukas Podolski

Born: *June 04, 1985, Gilwice, Poland*
Position: *Striker*
Squad Number: *9*
Previous Clubs: *Cologne, Bayern Munich, Cologne*
Joined Arsenal: *July 01, 2012*

A fast and precise forward player, Lukas has a fine eye for football and a magnificent left foot. His arrival at the Club was greeted enthusiastically by fans who were aware of his colossal achievements on the international stage. Lukas, who won his 100th cap for Germany at the record-breaking early age of 26, has a scoring record of nearly one in every two games at international level.

At club level, he announced his abilities early, scoring 51 goals in just 85 games during one campaign for Cologne. He has shown himself to be a versatile and whole-hearted player. The Premier League could prove a happy hunting ground for Lukas.

PLAYER PROFILES

MIKEL ARTETA

Born: March 26, 1982
San Sebastian, Spain
Squad number: 8
Position: Midfielder
Joined Gunners: August 31, 2011

When he arrived from Everton on transfer deadline day in August 2011, the young Spaniard carried considerable expectation. He had won the treble with Rangers in 2003 and been on the books of top European sides including Barcelona and Paris St Germain.

He did not disappoint, quickly adding consistency, class and style to the Gunners midfield. Few players are as reliable as Arteta, who is an accomplished and assured all-rounder. He and Song developed a fine understanding in the centre of the pitch, each covering one another's runs perfectly.

He has scored some important goals for the Gunners, including a free-kick against Aston Villa and a long-range stunner against Manchester City that sealed three vital points. He once said that his hope is that he can bring *"balance"* to the Arsenal team. He has more than succeeded in this aim.

MIKEL SAYS: *"I'm trying to contribute the best way to the team that I can. Scoring goals is not one of my most important jobs because we have better players in the team to do that. But it's always nice to help. As long as we keep winning, that's the most important thing."*

ARSÈNE WENGER SAYS:

For his goal against Manchester City, he first won the ball back, he then finished the action and scored the goal. That is what I call a real midfielder, a guy who is always in the game.

AARON RAMSEY

Born: December 26, 1990, Caerphilly, Wales

Squad number: 16

Position: Midfielder

Joined Gunners: June 13, 2008

aaron is the ultimate midfield maestro. He works hard, has superb levels of vision and technique, superb passing skills and a fine eye for goal. His energy, enthusiasm and professionalism are unrivalled. What more could one ask of a player?

He became a popular Gunner soon after he arrived from Cardiff City in 2008. Two years later he suffered a serious injury in the form of a broken leg but returned as good as ever, crowning his comeback with a cracking goal against Manchester United.

In 2011/12 he came to the fore in the centre of the park. With two highly rated midfielders having left the Club in the summer, immediately Ramsey grew in stature.

His composed and mature presence made his opponents shudder. He scored some fine goals, including against Tottenham, Marseille and Sunderland. Named the captain of Wales at the tender age of 21, Ramsey is quite a player.

AARON SAYS: *"I'm happy with what I've achieved so far, and especially with the way things are going for me personally but hopefully there's a lot more to come. What happened with my injury is behind me now, and I'm just really glad to be back playing for Arsenal regularly."*

ARSÈNE WENGER SAYS:

"I brought him in because of his quality. For me, he is growing month to month. I am very happy with what he is delivering and if Wilshere comes back they can play together."

THE CARLING CUP REVIEW

Arsenal v Shrewsbury Town

The Gunners kicked off their Carling Cup campaign hoping to put the ghosts of last season's final behind them and go one better. The game will always be remembered as the debut for Alex Oxlade-Chamberlain. He sealed a promising performance by scoring a long range effort that put the Gunners in front, after Shrewsbury's early lead had been cancelled out by Kieran Gibbs. The game, and Arsenal's passage to the next round, was sealed by another first goal – from Yossi Benayoun. Wenger's men showed great resilience in this tie and got their name in the hat for the next round.

Arsenal v Bolton Wanderers

Former Gunner Fabrice Muamba's strike early in the second-half heaped pressure onto the home side. Then two goals in three minutes from Andrey Arshavin, and a beautiful curling strike from Park Chu Young – his first goal for the Club – ensured Arsenal would be participating in the quarter-finals for a record 15th time. Wenger rested several first-team regulars and handed starts to young guns such as Yennaris, Miquel and Frimpong. All three impressed and showed that they can hold their own against the big teams, giving extra hope to the Gunners' faithful.

20 September, 2011
Arsenal 3-1 Shrewsbury
(Gibbs, Oxlade-Chamberlain, Benayoun)

25 October, 2011
Arsenal 2-1 Bolton Wanderers
(Arshavin, Young Park)

29 November, 2011
Arsenal 0-1 Manchester City

Arsenal v Manchester City

Arsenal's hopes of getting to Wembley for a second year running were dashed by a Sergio Aguero counter-attack goal seven minutes from time. A youthful Gunners side had impressed against the Premier League leaders and could have won the game were it not for some top class keeping from Pantilimon for the visitors. As extra-time seemed to loom, Arsenal pressed for a winner and were beaten on the break by City. It was, perhaps, the City line-up's superior age and experience showing. Arsenal could be proud of their achievements in the competition and left the pitch to a round of applause from both sets of fans.

TWEETING FOR ARSENAL!

By the end of the 2011/12 season, the Club's official Twitter account – launched in the summer of 2009 - had 1.5 million followers.

From Twitter takeovers to the players' individual accounts, here is everything you need to know about Arsenal's presence on the social networking website.

TWITTER TAKEOVERS!

During the 2011/12 season, the Club hosted a number of 'Twitter takeover' sessions. The sessions consisted of first-team players answering questions sent in via the Club's official Twitter account. These proved to be popular, informative and fun experiences.

Here are some highlights:

Wojciech Szczesny's favourite subject at school was history.

Wojciech Szczesny

What was your favourite subject at school?

'It was history, actually. I liked the teacher.'

Abou Diaby

Do you miss Highbury?

'A lot!'

Which sport other than football would you like to play?

'Basketball.'

Laurent Koscielny

Are you as good a dancer as Alex Song would lead us to believe?

'No. Alex Song has this in his body, I just look at Alex instead!'

Bacary Sagna's distinctive hairstyle is actually the result of a bet!

Bacary Sagna

What inspired your hairstyle?

'It was a bet with my father.'

What's your favourite food?

'Lebanese food - because it's quite healthy. There's a place near mine, so I go quite often.'

Aaron Ramsey

What are your tattoos of and what do they mean to you?

'There's a castle from where I am from in Wales, some religious tattoos as well. A passage from the bible, too.'

OFFICIAL ARSENAL ACCOUNTS:

Main Club account: @Arsenal
News from live events: @ArsenalLive
Johan Djourou: @johandjourou
Bacary Sagna: @Sagnaofficial
Jack Wilshere: @jack_wilshere
Alex Oxlade-Chamberlain: @Alex_OxChambo
Emmanuel Y Frimpong: @Frimpong26AFC
Conor Henderson: @Henderson_91

THE 100 CLUB!

Robin Van Persie scored his 99th and 100th goals for Arsenal Football Club against Bolton Wanderers on September 24, 2011. He is the 17th player to reach a century of Arsenal goals. Examine how he reached this magnificent milestone and find out who the other 16 players are in the Gunners 100 Club...

Robin's Century:

- His first goal was against Manchester City in the Carling Cup
- He scored his 100 in 238 matches – a rate of one goal per 2.38 appearances
- Of the 17 members of the 100 Club he is the 12th fastest to reach the century

His 100 goals came in the following competitions:

- 69 Premier League (2.35 games per goal)
- 17 in European matches (2.76 games per goal)
- Eight in the FA Cup (2 games per goal)
- Six in the League Cup (1.83 games per goal)

On reaching his century, he said:

'I know all about the history of the '100 Club', I know I'm No 17 and it's such a privilege to be part of Arsenal's history in that way – a real honour. When I had scored 82 or 83 goals I looked at the list and thought 'this is possible' and then I had such a good second half of last season that I knew if I stayed fit this season I would do it. It was just a big day for me, I'm so proud.''

The Gunners 100 Club in full	Dates	League	FA Cup	League Cup	Europe	Charity Shield	Total Goals	Total Apps	100th Goal Game
1. Thierry Henry	1999-2007	174	7	2	42	1	226	370	181
2. Ian Wright	1991-1998	128	12	29	15	1	185	288	143
3. Cliff Bastin	1929-1946	150	26	0	0	2	178	396	174
4. John Radford	1962-1976	111	15	12	11	0	149	481	306
5. Jimmy Brain	1923-1931	125	14	0	0	0	139	232	144
6. Ted Drake	1934-1945	124	12	0	0	3	139	184	108
7. Doug Lishman	1948-1956	125	10	0	0	2	137	244	163
8. Joe Hulme	1926-1938	107	17	0	0	1	125	374	307
9. David Jack	1928-1934	113	10	0	0	1	124	208	156
10. Dennis Bergkamp	1995-2006	87	14	8	11	0	120	423	296
11. Reg Lewis	1935-1953	103	13	0	0	2	118	176	152
12. Alan Smith	1987-1995	86	6	16	7	0	115	347	251
13. Jack Lambert	1926-1933	98	11	0	0	0	109	161	149
14. Frank Stapleton	1972-1981	75	15	14	4	0	108	300	276
15. David Herd	1954-1961	97	10	0	0	0	107	180	165
16. Joe Baker	1962-1966	93	4	0	3	0	100	156	152
17. Robin Van Persie	2004-	69	8	6	17	0	132	278	238

THE SEASON IN STATS!

A fan of Arsenal? A lover of numbers? Then you came to the right place. Here is a selection of super stats from the 2011/12 campaign, together with the final Premier League table for the season. Happy number-crunching, Gunners fans!

- Arsenal played 54 matches during the campaign;
- They qualified for the Champions League for the 15th successive season;
- They scored 96 goals;
- Conceded 67 goals;
- Kept 18 clean sheets, and
- Won 31 matches.

- 32 different players represented Arsenal in the Premier League, a Club record;
- Wojciech Szczesny (right) and Robin Van Persie (above) made the most overall appearances (48);
- Alex Song and Wojciech Szczesny made the most starts in Europe (9).

By the end of the season, the number of players who had appeared for the Club in its 125 year history was 803.

The final Premier League table 2011/12

POS	TEAM	P	W	D	L	F	A	+/-	PTS
1	Manchester City	38	28	5	5	93	29	64	89
2	Manchester United	38	28	5	5	89	33	56	89
3	**Arsenal**	**38**	**21**	**7**	**10**	**74**	**49**	**25**	**70**
4	Tottenham Hotspur	38	20	9	9	66	41	25	69
5	Newcastle United	38	19	8	11	56	51	5	65
6	Chelsea	38	18	10	10	65	46	19	64
7	Everton	38	15	11	12	50	40	10	56
8	Liverpool	38	14	10	14	47	40	7	52
9	Fulham	38	14	10	14	48	51	-3	52
10	W.B.A.	38	13	8	17	45	52	-7	47
11	Swansea	38	12	11	15	44	51	-7	47
12	Norwich	38	12	11	15	52	66	-14	47
13	Sunderland	38	11	12	15	45	46	-1	45
14	Stoke City	38	11	12	15	36	53	-17	45
15	Wigan Athletic	38	11	10	17	42	62	-20	43
16	Aston Villa	38	7	17	14	37	53	-16	38
17	QPR	38	10	7	21	43	66	-23	37
18	Bolton Wanderers	38	10	6	22	46	77	-31	36
19	Blackburn Rovers	38	8	7	23	48	78	-30	31
20	Wolverhampton Wanderers	38	5	10	23	40	82	-42	25

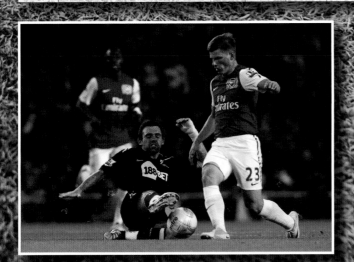

junior GUNNERS

It was another thrilling year for all members of Arsenal's young supporters club, the Junior Gunners.
Here are some highlights!

Camping on the Pitch!

400 Junior Gunners took part in the Camping on the Pitch event at Emirates Stadium. It was a thrilling experience for the boys and girls, aged between seven and twelve. First, they played on the hallowed turf, in matches arranged by the Club's community coaches. Then they dined in the exclusive Club level, watched the Champions League final on a big screen television and played table football. After all that, they slept in 200 two-person tents on the pitch. Club mascot Gunnersaurus was on hand to wish them all a good night's sleep.

Fabrice Muamba

Everyone involved with Arsenal were moved when Fabrice Muamba, who came through the ranks with Arsène Wenger's side, suffered a heart attack in a Bolton match at White Hart Lane in March 2012. The following weekend, Arsenal supporters unfurled a huge flag at the north end of Emirates Stadium and passed it over their heads, while chanting Muamba's name. "He is a loved guy," said Wenger of Muamba. "Because we have a young team, many of them grew up with Fabrice. There is a strong link when you fight together in the youth teams because it creates a special bond."

Know The Score!

Throughout the campaign, Junior Gunners competed in a score prediction game called Know the Score! The overall winner was Edwin See, who won the exciting prize of a photograph with the first team. Well played everyone – and well done Edwin!

...al Foundation

...al Foundation

...senal Football Club was
...ounce the launch of The
...on as part of the Club's 125th
...on. The Foundation is a grant-
...at focuses on work to motivate
...g people – often through
...ort –to help them
...tial and be the
...he charity will
...y for future
...e Arsenal
...a special
..." said
...cutive and
...e,

Podolski meets Gunnersaurus!

Everyone was excited when German international Lukas Podolski signed for the Club. As the ink was still drying on his contract, the forward was delighted to be introduced to Gunnersaurus.

...orters club, the Junior
...and girls from newborn
...pecial membership
...ance to attend
...layers throughout the
...can lead the team out at
...al mascots,

2011/12 MISCELLANY

Random facts and stats from the campaign...

Theo Walcott scored the Club's first Premier League goal for the second successive season.

The 5-3 win against Chelsea was the 500th victory of Arsène Wenger's reign.

Mikel Arteta scored the opening goal in three matches: against Blackburn Rovers, Wigan Athletic and Manchester City.

Robin van Persie averaged either a goal or assist every 81.9 minutes. He also scored 40.54 per cent of Arsenal's league goals.

The 3-2 victory at West Bromwich Albion was Pat Rice's final match as assistant manager at Arsenal. He first joined the Club as a player, 44 years previously.

Robin van Persie's match-winning volley against Everton was voted goal of the season, attracting 49 per cent of the votes cast in our fans' poll.

Robin van Persie was the top scorer with 37 goals. His nearest netter was Theo Walcott with 11.

Tomas Rosicky's goal against Tottenham Hotspur was his first in the league for more than two years.

In 29 of the games Laurent Koscielny appeared in, Arsenal conceded no more than one goal and kept 15 clean sheets.

Only Real Madrid and Manchester United can match Arsenal's achievement of being Champions League ever-presents since 1998/99.

Wojciech Szczesny was on the pitch for every minute of the Premier League campaign.

The 8-2 defeat by Manchester United was the heaviest defeat of Wenger's reign to date. The Frenchman described it as "terribly painful".

The grandchildren of Club founder David Danskin were present at the 125th anniversary celebrations, which took place on December 10, 2011.

Van Persie equalled the top flight record for scoring against 17 different teams in a single season.

During the season, the 2003/04 title winners, who went 49 games unbeaten, were voted the best team of the Premier League era.

Alex Song started more games than any other outfield player, and made the most goal assists.

Robin van Persie struck two hat-tricks: one against Chelsea and one against Blackburn Rovers.

Andrey Arshavin made the most appearances as a substitute. He was introduced during 14 matches.

LONDON OUR CITY

The highest attendance came against Chelsea in April, when 60,111 people watched.

GERVINHO

Born: May 27, 1987, Anyama, Ivory Coast

Squad number: 27

Position: Striker

Joined Gunners: July 18, 2011

The Ivorian forward arrived in north London in the summer of 2011 and quickly made an impression on the Arsenal faithful. His vigorous and wholehearted displays contributed a great deal to the campaign, with his goal against Blackburn Rovers in September an early taster of what he is capable of.

Ever since captaining his national side at under-21 level, Gervinho has been a fearsome figure on the international stage. He has proudly worn the shirt of the Ivory Coast at a World Cup, Olympic Games and Africa Cup of Nations. At each tournament he terrorised defences from across the globe.

Having adapted so seamlessly to the rigours of the English game in his first Premier League season, Gervinho is looking forward to good times ahead for the Gunners. The Arsenal fans will cheer him all the way.

GERVINHO SAYS: *"There is real hope that we can bring trophies to Arsenal. Every player is conscious of this and we're going to do all we can to achieve it this season."*

ARSÈNE WENGER SAYS:

" He was one of the signings of the summer when he came to England. His attitude, his work rate, his technical quality and the intelligence of his runs are absolutely fantastic. "

ALEX OXLADE-CHAMBERLAIN

Born: *August 15, 1993, Portsmouth*

Squad number: *15*

Position: *Striker*

Joined Gunners: *August 08, 2011*

Alex's debut was a true baptism of fire for the teenager. He came on as a substitute in the 8-2 defeat at Old Trafford, just a few weeks after he had joined the Club. His next two outings were far more enjoyable: he scored in the victories over Shrewsbury Town and Olympiacos at Emirates Stadium.

By the end of his first season with Arsenal, the young man known as 'The Ox', had become a firm favourite of the Gunners faithful. He also became a full England international, and took part in three of his country's four matches at Euro 2012.

Alex is the son of former England winger Mark Chamberlain. He became Southampton's second-youngest player - behind fellow Gunner Theo Walcott - in 2009/10. A player of great pace, considerable power and some grace, Alex is set to flourish even further in the years ahead. Both club and country will benefit.

ALEX SAYS: "I like to take people on and be an exciting player, that is just my game. Every time we step on to the pitch we are trying to do our best because we have a massive responsibility to try to get results."

ARSÈNE WENGER SAYS:

❝ Alex improved very quickly in his first season. He is a fighter as well, with personality, and is much more mature now. No wonder the fans love him. ❞

PLANET ARSENAL

The Gunners squad is a truly international affair.

Can you find your favourite player on this map?

01. Belgium
Thomas Vermaelen

02. Brazil
Andre Santos; Denilson

03. Costa Rica
Joel Campbell

04. Czech Republic
Tomas Rosicky

05. Denmark
Nicklas Bendtner

06. England
Theo Walcott; Alex Oxlade-Chamberlain; Jack Wilshere; Kieran Gibbs; Carl Jenkinson; Henri Lansbury

07. France
Arsène Wenger; Abou Diaby; Bacary Sagna; Laurent Koscielny; Sebastien Squillaci; Francis Coquelin; Marouane Chamakh; Olivier Giroud

08. Germany
Per Mertesacker

09. Ghana
Emmanuel Frimpong

10. Italy
Vito Mannone

11. Ivory Coast
Johan Djourou; Gervinho

12. Japan
Ryo Miyaichi

13. Poland
Lukasz Fabianski; Lukas Podolski; Wojciech Szczesny

14. Russia
Andrey Arshavin

15. South Korea
Ju Young Park

16. Spain
Manuel Almunia; Mikel Arteta; Santi Cazorla

17. Wales
Aaron Ramsey

TRIVIA QUIZ

3.

7.

STARTING AT THE BACK:

1. Which national team did David Seaman play for: England or Latvia?

2. What nationality is Wojciech Szczesny?

3. In which year did Johan Djourou join the Club?

4. True or false: Sebastien Squillaci once played for Mr Wenger's former club: AS Monaco.

5. How many Premier League goals did Arsenal concede in 2011/12?

6. Which defender joined Arsenal from Auxerre in July 2007?

7. What nationality is Club legend Tony Adams?

8. True or false: coach Steve Bould made 372 appearances for Arsenal.

9. What position does Lukasz Fabianski play in?

10. True or false: television pundits Martin Keown and Lee Dixon both played in defence for Arsenal.

MIDDLE CLASS:

1. What nationality is Aaron Ramsey?

2. Which other Premier League side has Mikel Arteta played for?

3. In which year did Tomas Rosicky join the Club?

4. Which midfielder scored in the 5-3 defeat of Chelsea?

5. And which midfielder scored against Marseille?

6. Which club did Santi Cazorla join the Gunners from?

7. In which country was Emmanuel Frimpong born?

8. Did Alex Song join the Gunners in 2005 or 2010?

9. True or false: Manchester City executive Patrick Viera won two Doubles with Arsenal.

10. Which club does former captain Cesc Fabregas now play for?

8.

2011/12 VICTORIES:

1. Which team did the Gunners record their first Premier League win of 2011/12 against?

2. Which team did Arsenal beat 7-1?

3. Which Italian side did the Gunners beat twice in the Champions League?

4. What was the score when Arsenal beat Tottenham Hotspur?

5. Who did the Gunners beat 3-2 on the final day of the season?

6. What was the score when Arsenal beat Aston Villa in the FA Cup?

7. In which competition did the Gunners beat Shrewsbury Town?

8. True or false: Arsenal beat Liverpool 1-0 at Anfield.

9. What was the score when Arsenal beat AC Milan at Emirates Stadium?

10. How many league matches did Arsenal win in 2011/12?

STRIKINGLY GOOD!

1. Against which team did Lukas Podolski score his first Premier League goal?

2. Ju Young Park has won the captain's armband for which national side?

3. Which south coast side have Theo Walcott and Alex Oxlade-Chamberlain played for?

4. Which striker joined Arsenal from French side Lille in 2011?

5. Marouane Chamakh plays for Morocco or Mauritius?

6. Who was the second highest scorer for 2011/12?

7. And how many goals did he score?

8. What age was Alex Oxlade-Chamberlain when he joined the Southampton Academy?

9. Which French player joined the Gunners for a second time during 2011/12?

10. Who is the Club's second-highest goal-scorer of all time?

Answers on Page 61

1.

CLUB HISTORY:

1. In which year did Arsene Wenger join the Club?

2. Against which team did Ian Wright break Cliff Bastin's goal-scoring record: Bolton Wanderers or Cowdenbeath?

3. Which Manager was appointed in 1925?

4. And which Manager was at the helm between 1986 and 1995?

5. In which year did the Gunners last win the Premier League?

6. Arsenal won the Double in 1971, 1998 and which other year?

7. In which year did Arsenal leave Highbury?

8. Name the team that Arsenal beat in the 1993 FA Cup and League Cup Finals.

9. What nationality is Dennis Bergkamp?

10. True or false: The Gunners beat Southampton in the 2003 FA Cup Final.

ROSSWORD

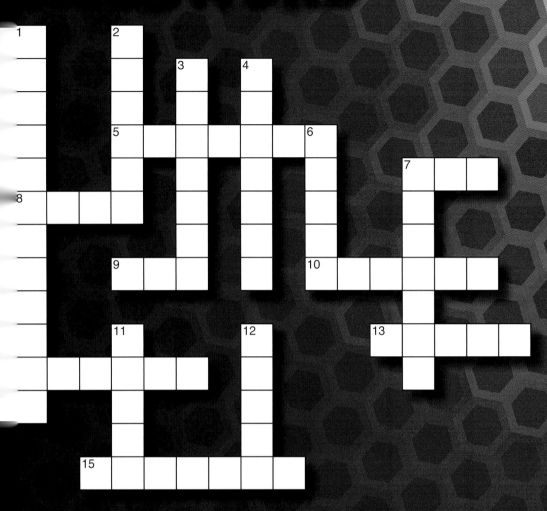

SPOT THE
DIFFERENCE

Can you spot all
of the 8 differences
in the pictures below?

Answers on Page 61

A.

B.

CHARTING THE PROGRESS...

Use this chart to refer back to key moments in the 2011/12 season, and keep it up-to-date with the equivalent moments in the 2012/13 campaign. Enjoy!

PREMIER LEAGUE 2011/12 — 2012/13

	2011/12	2012/13
FINAL POSITION	3RD	
FIRST HOME WIN	V SWANSEA 1-0	
FIRST AWAY WIN	V CHELSEA 5-3	
FIRST HOME DRAW	V FULHAM 1-1	
FIRST AWAY DRAW	V BOLTON 0-0	

DOMESTIC CUPS 2011/12 — 2012/13

	2011/12	2012/13
FA CUP	FIFTH ROUND: SUNDERLAND	
CARLING CUP	QUARTER FINALS: MANCHESTER CITY	

CHAMPIONS LEAGUE PROGRESS 2011/12 — 2012/13

	2011/12	2012/13
FIRST HOME WIN	UDINESE 1-0	
FIRST AWAY WIN	UDINESE 2-1	
FIRST HOME DRAW	MARSEILLE 0-0	
FIRST AWAY DRAW	BORUSSIA DORTMUND 1-1	

FIRST GOALS IN 2011/12 — 2012/13

	2011/12	2012/13
PREMIER LEAGUE	WALCOTT V MANCHESTER UNITED	
FA CUP	THIERRY HENRY V LEEDS UNITED	
CARLING CUP	KIERAN GIBBS V SHREWSBURY TOWN	

QUIZ ANSWERS

TRIVIA QUIZ – PAGES 56 & 57

Starting at the Back

1. England
2. Polish
3. 2003
4. True
5. 49
6. Bacary Sagna
7. English
8. True
9. Goalkeeper
10. True

Middle Class

1. Welsh
2. Everton
3. 2006
4. Andre Santos
5. Aaron Ramsey
6. Malaga
7. Ghana
8. 2005
9. True
10. Barcelona

Strikingly Good!

1. Liverpool
2. South Korea
3. Southampton
4. Gervinho
5. Morocco
6. Theo Walcott
7. 11
8. Seven
9. Thierry Henry
10. Ian Wright

2012/12 Victories:

1. Swansea City
2. Blackburn Rovers
3. Udinese
4. 5-2
5. West Bromwich Albion
6. 3-2
7. Carling Cup
8. False: the score was 2-1 to Arsenal
9. 3-0
10. 21

History

1. 1996
2. Bolton Wanderers
3. Herbert Chapman
4. George Graham
5. 2004
6. 2002
7. 2006
8. Sheffield Wednesday
9. Dutch
10. True

CROSSWORD – PAGE 58

Across

5. Belgium
7. Ten
8. Rice
9. Net
10. Ninety
13. Grass
14. Gunners
15. Chelsea

Down

1. Gunnersaurus
2. Double
3. Walcott
4. Udinese
6. Milan
7. Thierry
11. Welsh
12. Three

SPOT THE DIFFERENCE – PAGE 59

WHERE'S
GUNNERSAURUS?